Sex, Drugs & Spoken Word

Mix Tape Collection III

Jason Brain

Poetry In Motion
Publishing House

CHAPBOOKS INCLUDED IN THIS COLLECTION:

The Shape of Pomes to Come
Mix Tape #8

You Don't Know Me (You're Welcome)
Mix Tape #9

Relationshit
Mix Tape #10

Thoughts of a Lost Dreamer
Mix Tape #11

Written, Revised, Organized, and Designed by Jason Brain

Front cover photo by Jason Brain
Back cover photo by Peter Chagnon

Poetry In Motion Publishing House
Los Angeles, CA

Copyright © 2019 Jason Brain

ISBN-13: 978-0-9916053-5-4

All Rights Reserved

No part of this publication may be reproduced or transmitted in any form or by any means, electronic or mechanical, including photocopying, recording, or by any information storage and retrieval system without the prior written consent of the publisher

First Edition

DEDICATION

To my wife
Crystal

For all the inspiration
For better or worse

May the inkwell
Never dry

The Shape of Pomes to Come

Mix Tape #8

Mix Tape #8
The Shape of Pomes to Come

Under The Influence

One Thought

Reclined & Dimed

Drowned In Ink

Write!?

Baby Girl Supernova

Wonder, Keep Me Younger

The Last Cloud

Secrete

The Wild Hours

Full Moon

One More Round

Infinite Words

Remember Stars

Sky Full Of Wonder

Don't Think Once

No Fun, Just Fucks

Poems To Fuck To

Moving On, Next

Stand Bye

Good For Them

Go

Never Finished

Under The Influence

It all started in the summer of 1994

I had just turned nine years old
And I was in search of a feeling

Something more than I could touch, instead
I needed something
To believe in

And there I found it, all on a Green Day
Welcome to Paradise, this *American Idiot*
Finding out *Nice Guys Finish Last*

And it was then that my *Semi-Charmed Life*
Began to fully bloom beneath the *Tattoo of the Sun*
Only to find my Third Eye Blind
Being born at the right hand of the Boss, Bruce Springsteen
Just before *Closing Time*, I was feeling so Semisonic
Like *Santeria*, Sublime

Acting wild and out like an Arctic Monkey
The View From The Afternoon reassured me
I Bet You Look Good On The Dancefoor, girl

Still, *I Hate To Say I Told You So* they all said
But The Hives, they give everyone that same itch

So I swallowed my pride, I choked on the rind
I flipped *Inside Out* when I bit hard into the apple of Eve 6

You see, no longer was I to be just another *Refugee*
Tom Petty-ing around, waiting for my *American Girl*

No, the purpose of my Operation Ivy is to discover
I don't know nothing, because *Knowledge* is my energy
And all I'll ever need is my *Sound System*

Yet abused and Refused, *The Shape of Punk to Come*
Blasting out The (International) Noise Conspiracy
Opened my mind, while *Capitalism Stole My Virginity*

But it was no matter, you see, I was already downing shot
After sucker punch of Everclear, going blind
Becoming *Everything to Everyone* on *Santa Monica* & Vine

Lit like a *Roman Candle,* Elliott Smith was whispering unto me
From a *Basement On The Hill* to just *Say Yes*

Thankfully for me
By the time I opened my third eye wide
I had already been tuned into a new *Cosmic Thing*
One that B-52'd Van Morrison into *The Wind*

A Cat Stevens searching for a *Moonshadow* to hide itself within
Alongside *The Pretender, Dancing In The Dark*

Quieter than an action Jackson Browne, making his move
On the sweetest *Brown Sugar, Like a Rolling Stone*
Only getting higher on the best damn *Dope Show*
Bob Dylan and Marilyn Manson never got to go to
With A Boy Named Sue no matter how much
Johnny Cash they'd saved selling lemonade to *My Generation*
Because, although *The Kids Are Alright*
The parents are always like
"The Who!?" again

I had found it

Nine years old with something to believe in
So innocent, under the influence: I'm still addicted

Because there's no time to stop, no thought for pause
Life is meant to be lived out loud

Just ... press ...
Play

One Thought

One poem
One stanza
One line
One word

Only takes
One thought
In an instant
To change the world

You were born ready
To be that moment

Some would say
Thought is danger
Speak no truth
Quiet blues
Action uncouth

I say I want
An honest life
Painful and subjective
Personal and infectious

One truth every line
One slice deeper each time

Takes one blink
Fleeting and feeling
Like a scent undefined
To change a life

Where will you be
As the breeze
Passes by?

Reclined & Dimed

Stop leaning on everything, kid
Gonna get yourself killed out there
Resting the weight of your trust
On inanimate energy at will

Bear the burden of being alone
Alongside everyone else, child
Upright and on both feet
Trudging uphill on both sides

You're not going to be a barista forever
You know you're destined for something greater than a grande
It's just a matter of dreams between days
Taking punches with grace

May not be fame
May not be fortune
May not be exactly like
Your bleeding heart expects

Stand tall, young adult
A 12oz coffee is still a small
There is no such thing as a free laugh
That's no way to ready yourself for attack

Stop leaning on everything, man
Off balance, you're fresh meat waiting to fall
The future's brutal, at best
Sights been set on you since your name was called

Gonna take a lot more than caffeine
To survive this thing called breathing

You're more than a capital machine
You're 100-percent human being

Drowned In Ink

I roll my sleeves back
To write poetry

Don't need
Blood splashing
Up my arms
Giving me away

Only a writer who wants to get caught
Leaves a clue to find

Beyond expression
Ink is poison
Seeping into the crevices
Between the surface and the skin
Turning insides out
Burning bones to ash

'Tis better to be stained by life than never stained at all?

What are we waiting for?
What are we holding back?
Words will find their way to daylight
Whether you fight, deny or write

How fast's your hook?
How deep's your well?

I roll my sleeves back to write poetry
Snap my gloves with sinister satisfaction

Like a good criminal boy scout
I leave no trace

Scene scrubbed of all evidence
Only my muses' fingerprints remain

Write!?

I don't write anymore
I fucking live now, and it's horrible!
Don't do it!
Avoid it at all costs
Write more
Before they tell you no more ideas
Before they eat you alive
You're delicious, by the way; stay delicious
Keep your head up and wits about you
Lot of dumb shits out there
Spouting charisma as wisdom nowadays
But I ain't with them, rift right through 'em
Sift through the garden of my mind
Weeding all the negativity and bullshit I can find
Baby, Buddha's got me grounded
Ganja's got me lifted
Pen in hand I write my wrongs
And work past my futures unwritten
Because there's whole days flying by
Before I sign another haiku penned just for you
It's crazy, I'm crazy right?
Write?
Why would I do something as dangerous as that?
The man's on a mission to disarm the citizens
Keep the ink in the pen and cage inside the men
Do you know how many years in prison I'd be given
If every thing I thought was found written?
Hell, can't even speak my forbidden fruit
Without raising a few disconcerted red flags
Write?
Who does *that* anymore?
There's got to be a robot that can do it now
Fast! Faster! Fasterest!
And then what!?
Don't look down
Just write now

Baby Girl Supernova

Baby girl, you are my entire world
I melt on the ice by the fire in your eyes

You see, you complete me
I thought I knew myself completely
Until, baby girl, you became the key to my destiny's door
Unlocking new possibilities unimaginable
From the bitter sobriety of adulthood

Sure, these nights are no laughing matter
Still, you fill my lungs with light, just the sight of your smile
Lying in my arms nestled tight from sunset to sunrise
I delight every moment you are alive in my life

Baby girl, you are my entire world

Actually
Excuse me, baby girl
You have become my entire universe

Nothing compares to the gravity of your heartbeat
How it grips me from reality, always brings me back to you

Supernova, show me no mercy upon maturation
I want to experience the full wonder of your love

It's truly impossible to put into words
How remarkably, instantly, inexplicably
You rocked my worthless world, because
Before you now, nothing really mattered
All energy exhausted for another buck?

No longer

Rose gold quartz pumps through my veins
Pure starlight shines up and down my spine
Illuminating my brain, enlightening my mind

And I can't find greater motivation than
Your little hand 'round my pinkie tight

To think
Some men
Take advantage
Of the privilege
This whole
Fatherhood-thing is

Baby girl
My supernova
Show me
No mercy

You're going to grow up
Larger
Than my arms will carry
Only time will tell
When you no longer need
My help
Whether I like it
Or not

Supernova
My baby girl

How about this
You teach me a new trick or two along the way
And I will lay all my loving wisdom
Down upon you

And when all else fails
Do remember this

Go ask mom

Wonder, Keep Me Younger

I could live another 50 more years
Off the magic in your young wonder

Out of thin air and into the daytime
Bouncing off every molecule in sight
How it ignites neurons of enlightenment
Once held in my spirit, long forgotten

Watching drops of rain water
Race across the car windows
Amazed and entertained

Learning about deaths mysteries
Saddened and mystified
In the same state

Playing with light in your eye
Squinting, open wide, how it shines
In and out like the tide

I try to soak in these waves of humility
As they wash over me, reborn in your vision
My children, how you remind me of our spirit
Where mysticism and innocence meet

A playful wisdom
Few hold on to
Past adolescence
Into, through the fire

Stay young, my love
Keep wonder
Seek magic daily
And hold tight

Innocence fades
Painfully quiet

The Last Cloud

Most scientists agree
We're as fucked as fucked can be

100 percently as a matter of factly

The temperature keeps rising
And politicians keep fighting
The cold hard truth: Life on Earth is dying
Faster than unions and lightning strike

The last cloud floats lonely tonight

Mother Earth weeps through eyes inside the noose
Seconds separate the drop and the pardon call
Moments we no longer have to waste
Dominoes stacked to fall

The last deciduous to green
The last fruit to flower
The last seed and root
The last breath we see

Was it worth all the commercial advertising?

Can you believe mere meters of leaves and needles
Have created miles of atmosphere
And here humanity is replying to the planet's cries
Like, 'New phone, who dis?'

100% of scientists agree
You can fuck yourself mightily
If you're one grain greater the problem
Than the solution we're seeking

Save your pollution
Spare me your condolences
Stake a claim in your godforsaken humanity

VIII: The Shape of Pomes to Come

Stand for an end greater than your selfish means

Mother Earth weeps beneath our feet
But still, we've got seconds to spare
If we care to make one decided effort

Enlightenment strikes like lightening
In all forms of weather

Believe in miracles
Like there's no tomorrow

There's no tomorrow
Guaranteed

The last cloud floats alone lonely

Secrete

As oils rise to the surface of my blood
I can't help but bask in the bliss
Of a kiss from your sun
Shine

The Wild Hours

Capture the wild hours in little glass mason jars
Store them for good luck on sunny window sills, or
Safely upon the tiny shelves of your bathroom

They are so fleeting
The wild hours

If you happen upon a few without mason jars near
Use your wild hands, wild arms and hold onto them
As long as humanly possible, my dear
Just not too tight

They are delicate
The wild hours

If you're able to catch a few every week
Consider yourself blessed
You've put yourself in position
For a life of beauty and purpose

They are karmic
The wild hours

For when you cannot find a few wild hours in nature
The soul must draw the wild from your blood
And unless you're immortal, good luck
There's limits to your wild well

We are human
We wild ones

It's never too late to start
Capture a few wild hours soon
Before the wild hours
Devour you whole

Full Moon

Ride her wave of ecstasy
Rise and fall with her moans
Bury your hands deep into her bones
Hold on for dear death

She's an animal of a goddess
Her kiss more dangerous than her bite

She'll consume you
Completely

She'll spit you out
With the rest

She's more than a force of nature
She's Mother Nature, herself
She's ready to destroy everything
Everyone who denies her siren sting

Accept your fate, weary romantics
Can't let these juicy waves get away

Catch her before her fury disappears
These women don't roll in every day

One More Round

She walks in like rock 'n roll
Red high heels riding hips like lightening

Most deer get froze
Caught in the gaze of her fire tail
Phoenix blazing behind her pirate sails

I can't help but spend
One moment lost in the thought
Of how she gets down
After a few drinks out on the town
Around midnight
Where inhibitions and intuitions collide
Like a man intent on destruction
Wondering where he went
Lost in that thought

She walks up like the second coming of rock n' roll
Wearing red hot high heels with hips crashing like thunder
Like she owns the place, every damn door she enters

I can't help but to think for one more moment
Before it's just the headlights of reality and me
Dancing in the dark high on desolation
I can't help but think I'm delusional

Our eyes meet, and for one moment
I can truly see
Her

She walks on
Past me, writing my poetry
Drinking my beer and whiskey by the bar

Pen in one hand
Cock in the other

Infinite Words

One handful of words can be more powerful
Than a military complex of bombs

The threat doesn't lie in the ink
The danger rises from a single idea
One photo is worth one-thousand words
One word is liable to start one-thousand revolutions

A handful of sexy words got me laid
A handful of ripe words got me paid
A handful of wise words got me raised
And to this day, I'll never be the same
As I was, when I was, only yesterday

It's not the game, it's the grammar
Not the function, it's the form
No, it's not the meaning, it's the in-between
This isn't a battle of wits in this world
Where words are war
Actions speak more

But believe you me that a handful of 'em
Shaken and stirred, poured just right
Has the power to destroy the world for the better
Any given open mic night

One muse, one mind, one thought
In the blink of an eye

Speak up!
Wield your words with might
Before someone louder
Shuts you down for good

Leave nothing left unsaid

Do not go silent into that free write

Remember Stars

Remember stars?

Do you, at least
Remember reading
About them
In history class?

I bet they were beautiful

I've heard they are what we are born of
I've also heard they are gigantic balls of gas

Who am I to judge?

Days too digital
Nights so fluorescent
Feels unnatural

Guess we'll never know
Any better
Anymore
Anyway

Sky Full Of Wonder

The sky is full of color

It only looks so blue so often

Reds bleed through everything
Blues into purples, yellows to greens
And oranges to anything

And right now
The sun has just set

And while it may not be
Shining directly on me
Light still resides
In my sky

The horizon reminds me
My mind is full of wonder

That my life, like my sky
Is not black and white, no
I am full of color

Life is lived
Dance to it
Be free

Wander along the cusp of day
Find the hues of life
In the shadows
Of the night

Don't Think Once

Don't think twice
They'll eat you alive
The world is on the hunt
She's hungry for spines

Don't ask me why, but
I think we've run out of time
Not that there's a countdown set
We've just overstayed our visit
No one wants inconsiderate shits
As guests in home or business

If only compassion was the answer
Instead of comfortable apathy

Get up off your knees and wipe your chin
Capitalism's sauce is convenient, not cuisine
Unplug your cocks and tits for one minute
Inconvenience my ego to enlightenment

Civilization crumbles
Past your selfie lens
Busy scrolling the feed
Tightening the noose ends

Go with the flow
Before you're not swallowed
But spit out whole

Back into reality every morning
From dreams stolen
And futures sold

Don't think twice
Nature don't think once

No Fun, Just Fucks

I don't write poetry for fun
Just for fucks

Like, fuck you
And fuck its, too
Mother-fuckers
And fucking shits
Fucking assholes
Fucking fucks
Fucks for fuck sake
And your fucking face

Fucking days, fucking nights
Fucking kids, fucking wife
Fucking job, fucking chores
Fucking bills, fucking wars

I don't write fucking poetry
I seduce imagination into fucking existence

From the fucking ether comes a fucking thought
That mind-fucks meaning into word-fucking-images
Vibrating off my tongue to your fucking senses
Blowing your virgin brain as my ideas fuck your insides

This isn't fun, this is fucks

One ring along the great fucking chain of inspiration
I write in fuck-ink ecstasy for your pleasure, fucker
I take this poetic responsibility very fucking seriously

Obviously

What did you expect?
Fucking poetics?

What makes you so fucking great?

Poems To Fuck To

I want to write poetry more seductive than roses
More intoxicating than money, any luxury
I want to compose the words that turn you on

Labia linguistics between your thighs
Tongue tied right 'round your lips
I quip every time I find you
Riding my stanzas again, cowgirl

I want to write poetry to fuck to

No beating 'round the bush
Your tush walking my way
Has got me going crazy, wondering
How hard it drops, how it gets down
And in these thoughts, drowning
I'm pounding pavement, growing stronger
Defying physics to envisage pure bliss
Written in hot breath and ink sweat on my mattress

Every glimmer of your eyes has got
My fingertips holding on for dear life
Girl, you've got something stunning, and
I'm coming for you with weapons of loving

Words are incapable of expressing
What an orgasm your visage is

I want to write poetry to fuck to

I want to lie you down upon a bed of sonnets
Tease your iambic nature, kiss you all over in free verse
Senses blindfolded, I want to write
Poetry to fuck madly, passionately, haphazardly to

In words no one else's ears have ever heard
I want to write poems to fuck you to

Moving On, Next

Sometimes you've got to trust the devil
Sometimes you aught to kill the Buddha
Sometimes you want to do both at the same time
And at the same time, sometimes, you do

Sometimes, we do get sore
And sometimes, we do feel pain
Sometimes, we get ourselves into the strangest situations
And sometimes, we inflict disdain

Sometimes the path is ours, set just before us
Now for the making, this moment's here for the taking
Until we look around and find we need a vacation (tell me)
Who here needs a vacation?!?!

Because I've been here before-before
Same damn man I've been too many times and more
Same damn man, the same damn man
Too many times and more

We continue to kill time so long as time kills us
Just doing with us as it wills while we just do nothing
Cuz everyone's fucked; just give it all up
No love about it for you or your favorite stuffed animal

We're spilling life as life spills us, pouring
Dust into the wind from the skin we've shed, breathed in again
Everyone's reborn in the flame every fucking day
And this is a new game we're playing, cooler than unusual

Right inside your heart's a pyre of memories and emotions
Burning us up, burning us down, and burning us out
And to think, you used to call this town your home (tell me)
What do you call it now?

Because I've been here before-before
Same damn man I've been too many times and more

VIII: The Shape of Pomes to Come

Same damn man, the same damn man
Too many times and more

On the unyielding road of life, you let one in
And they let another, and they another, and
Before you know it, there you are; left behind
Sometimes you aught to just change lanes, but
Who's to blame (no one) that's who (truth)

We're all passengers in the drivers seat, the rear view
Steered by a voice without form down the darkest roads
Just before sunrise, under the most colorful skies before sunset
Headed west passing through physical states and beyond
Onto interstates into inner-states of being, human and divine

On the unforgiving road of life, skid marks last longer
Than the tires that left them, as asphalt paves way
Towards on and off ramps rented, dejected; like an Aston Martin
Stuck behind a Harley, the stakes get gnarly (tell me)
Shouldn't you get started?

Because I've been here before-before
Same damn man I am, is, are, was were
To be is to be not
And so I bow

In the face of ignorance, with every love wish
To those who need it and those who deserve it
I bow

On your death bed, upside down on my head
Both hands tied behind my back, or gun in lap
I bow

There's no time like now, no worries about how
With or without the tao, like it's my last chance (might as well)
Bow

Stand Bye

Quiet
On

There
Still

One red light
No other sign

Everything in standby
Right nearby
Everything in standby
Left nearby

Silent
Off

Blank
Blinking

Disconnect
Connected

Everything in standby
Right nearby
Everything in standby
Left nearby

Close
Steady

Quick
Ready

On
Off
On

VIII: The Shape of Pomes to Come

Everything in standby
Right nearby
Everything in standby
Left right nearby

Consuming energy
Right beneath our eyes
Vampires at every outlet
One drop of blood at a time

On
Off

On

Good For Them

Good for all the fools
Who pomp and profess of knowing themselves completely

Good for all the fucks
Who work tirelessly to kick up dust and run amuck indiscreetly

Good for all the fakes
Who run their mouths, act all cool, silly actors spoiling reality TV

Good for them all
I hope they're happy
Living in their little world

Who knew talentlessness
Could look so aspiring
To the uncritical eye

She's more a state of mind
Than a place to raise a consciousness

Los Angeles, you whore
The things you're willing to do
For your fifteen minutes of fame

It's a shame
All the fools, fucks, and fakes
You've taken, forsaken

For their sake
May you raise them up
Off their quivering knees
Souls still in place

To all who come to LA with a dream and a face
I hope you get what you came for
In vain

Go

Initiate
Deviate
Resuscitate, then
Re-create

It's time to escape

Stimulate
Intoxicate
Indoctrinate, then
Inoculate

It's time to escape now

Individuate
Imaginate
Concentrate, then
Re-evaluate

It's time to escape now
Go

As fast as you can
As far as your legs will get you

Run

It's time to escape
Your untimely fate
The grief of life's strain
Death's nearing date
There's no time to wait

You blink twice
You're already reborn
Once again
Institutionalized

Never Finished

One more poem
One more stanza
One more line
One more word
The work's complete
Says me
Settling, compromising
On another word
Another line
Another stanza
Another poem
Better saved
For never

[Turn book to Mix Tape #9]

You Don't Know Me (You're Welcome)

Mix Tape #9

Mix Tape #9
You Don't Know Me (You're Welcome)

Like Wine (Better Man)

What Have You

Resilience (And Still So Far To Go)

Son, Father, Holy Spirit

Balanced Equation

You Don't Know Me (You're Welcome)

Sex, Drugs & Spoken Word

Athletix

Karaoke Night

Caffeinding

Pick Me Up

Another Round, Please

Titties

Tantra Goddess*

One Orgasm Per Day

I Don't Mind

Paper, Please

Prospects & Opportunities

Hurt

Simulacrum

One Hundred Years Or Bust

"Tantra Goddess" & "Titties" 1st appeared in Poems To F*ck To (2015)
by Poetry In Motion Publishing House

IX: You Don't Know Me (You're Welcome)

Like Wine (Better Man)

Of course I could be better than I am

I'm just a boy
Finding out
What it takes
To be a man

Like wine
We're getting better
All the time

To decay by design's another tale
We're taught to memorize, but
We lovers denounce that line

Destinations don't come with instructions, no
Every year, I fear, I feel I'm taking another step up and forward
But in a life built up of innumerable stories
Another step's another drop in the bucket
So stay up, I'm doing my best
To be better

Hope to prove gravity's a figment of our imaginations
Friction's a pigment of the sounds our mouths are making

So lo and behold, I don't announce every time I do differently
Choose to rise to my occasion every time such opportunities arise

This is a battle I'm fighting
Deep within, a war I'm waging
Against myself, for myself
For the world
At large

When I was five
I learned my abc's

At seven

I learned what it's like
To be another human being

At nine
I discovered everyone
One day will die

When I was eleven
I learned about . . . girls

When I was thirteen
I learned about . . . myself

At fifteen
I briefly experienced
Peace

At seventeen
I learned I know
Nothing really

At nineteen
I learned the ways of the world
In theory

At twenty-one
I uncovered the secrets
Behind my dreams

And when I was twenty-three
I finally learned how
To breathe

Don't pull me from the vine before I'm fully ripe
I'm just a boy in this life trying to get it right finally

Nobody ever said it was going to be easy, then again
Everybody's looking out for number one

Of course I could be better than I am

IX: You Don't Know Me (You're Welcome)

Consider me human
Being

Like wine
I am
Getting better
All the time

One step
After the last
One step
Before the next

Like wine
In the cellar
I'm ripe
And patient
Like life
For the taking
I'm waiting on you
To taste this life
With me

Let's raise a glass
In honor of yesterday
In anticipation of tomorrow
Here always

Cheers

What Have You

I wear pants that fit; aren't a size too skinny
I wear glasses with real lenses in them; prescription
My beanie is signature; not seasonal
My chronic; bomb since college
Vegan; my choice
Poet; a higher calling

I'm a young man on a mission
I'm not one to fuck around, but
I've been known to fuck around
If you're fucking with my business

Don't call me hipster
Don't call me hippie
Don't call me human
Save it for my eulogy

I've got doors to destroy
Ceilings to crash
All while you label me
What have you
Not

IX: You Don't Know Me (You're Welcome)

Resilience (And Still So Far To Go)

And still so far to go

I repeat these lines to myself
When times get tough

And still so far to go

A constant, ceaseless reminder
I am blessed to be here, where I am
Discovering karma's sycophantic smile
Knows no bounds

Seeking future rainbows
Before todays clouds even rain
Fruits borne before the seeds are sown
From an earth born of fire; a cosmic fire
Similar to the one in our guts
One we refuse to confront

And still so far to go

Sticking to the some-what schedule
Venturing into moments unconsoled
Innocent, always beginning tomorrow
Five minutes early, a savior and a sinner
I'll become whatever's necessary this moment
I'm still not out of this fight alive just yet, alright

Everyone's got some chip on their shoulder
Some of us just happen to carry boulders
We carry on

We are resilient
We human beings

We've still so far to go

Alongside past generations

One of the few things left in common
Birth, death, the great unknown

Riding our coattails
Right in front of our face
Everywhere we look
Everywhere we don't

I bring myself back
Repeat my mantra of perseverance
Remind myself once and again
There is only now

And still so far to go

IX: You Don't Know Me (You're Welcome)

Son, Father, Holy Spirit

I don't believe
Jesus was the only son of god

I believe we all are the sons and daughters of god

I don't believe
Jesus was the messiah

I believe Jesus was the greatest shaman alive

I don't believe
Jesus was born immaculately

I believe all children are born without original sin

I believe
Jesus was a man
And love conquers all

I believe there's Jesus-, Buddha- nature in all of us
I believe we all have the power to work miracles
I believe Jesus nurtured his essence, energy, and spirit

The power we could harness
Finding silence inside us
Would open energy pathways
Bring a new conscious
To collective minds

I believe
Jesus was a man
Tapped into the universe
Divine

And you can too

Let's try

Balanced Equation

A fine blend of caffeine and cannabis
Ink and blood, beer and semen
Late nights and early mornings
Perseverance and procrastination

Learning harder, working smarter
Purveyor of linguistics and cunnalingus
Catholic upbringing and Taoist understanding
Speaking easy, thinking devious

Karaoke hijinks and library kinks
Nonfiction history and poetic philosophies
Soft-spoken anarchy amid screams for critical thinking
Type New Roman and cursive shorthand

Discontented in expectation and ready for anything
Incredibly injury prone parallel parking professional
Public introvert, solitary confinement extrovert
Drunk on deep breaths, high on groundedness

It doesn't always make sense
I just do my best
To find harmony between extremes
I'm just being me

You Don't Know Me (You're Welcome)

You don't know me
You're welcome

I'm a whole lot to handle
More than you can grasp
With physical forces alone

I am the dynamite
Ready to control and explode
At a moments notice, though
Not unprovoked

You poke the bull
You get the horns
Even kindergarteners know
Such laws of nature

You don't know me
You're welcome

It's best for your safety
Your sanity, no less
It's best you keep good distance
Or else you too may go do something crazy
Like fall in love or daydream regularly

I'm an airball waiting to happen
Into a basket six feet below
I'm more trouble than some'd say I'm worth
But maybe so are they also

Don't mind me
I dance for no reason
And once that becomes crime
We'll incite revolution
Anarchy's institutions

You don't know me

You're welcome

Hell bent, heaven sent
We all get our own means in the end

This is only the beginning
New rooms with old consequence

Every entrance we make
Nothing remains the same

Maybe, I'm just going insane

Breaking ballpoint pens
Every time I write with passion
Don't fight the creative tide
Add the damage to the budget
Avoid writers rations at all costs
Might do something crazy
Like get paid for this
Maybe

It's my grave, baby
Can you dig it?

You don't know me
I'm sorry

Sex, Drugs & Spoken Word

It's what I live for
What I live on

I'm a slut
A junkie
A beat
For a taste
Of dopamine
All over me

In only so many words and ways
With still so far to go
Leave me alone
I'll find my way home

Fantastic
Ecstatic
Linguistic

Turn me on! Turn me up! Turn me loose!

I've got sex
Drugs, and
Spoken word
Waiting for me
Within every breath
On the astral plane
I consecrate daily
Intoxicated, baby

How else
Would I pass
My days living
As I die every time
I remember my
Mortality

Passion before pleasure

Sex, Drugs & Spoken Word

Horse before the carriage

Sex
Drugs
Spoken word
Get me lifted
In ways and words
The mundane
Could only envision

Pure bliss
I exist
Within
Without

How do I come down
When my physical
Is the only body
Touching ground

Burning up
Fuel for lifetimes
Burning down
Karmic death timelines

I insist you take a moment sometime today
To imbibe on something other than burnt coffee or refined sugars

Give me
Sex, drugs, and spoken word
In no particular order
Any combination you've got the constitution for

It's why I live, how I'll die
In no particular order

Let's get high

IX: You Don't Know Me (You're Welcome)

Athletix

I'm addicted to ESPN

It's not my fault
I'm just a sports fanatic
Seeking athletics everywhere
24/7

Fútbol, baseball, basketball, hockey
American football, tennis, volleyball, golf
Rugby, racing, mixed martial arts, boxing
Swimming, track & field, wrestling, pool
Cricket, X-games, gymnastics, bowling and beyond

I want it all
All the time
All the sports
Lay it on me

Underdogs down to the wire
Clutch heroics under pressure
Nil-nil defensive battles
I want 'em all

Wasn't my fault I entered high school
Five-foot-nothing, a-hundred-barely-something

Truth be told, one of my greatest accomplishments
Is piercing our high school jerk-ass varsity quarterback
In an impromptu shit-talk throw off after sophmore P.E. class
With two daggers to my receiver through his coverage
To an over throw by him and pass defensed by me

You name it, I'll play it
In a perfect world I'd be playing from sunrise to bedtime

Instead, I get my fix straight from Bristol, Connecticut
Easiest way to get my hit

Karaoke Night

I enter the bar: Karaoke
1st drink: Jameson neat, quick

2nd drink: Pint of Miller Lite
Cheapest draught they got

3rd drink: Her eyes
Deer in headlights

4th drink: Her voice
Who knew there was a part of you
Sexier than those eyes

5th drink: Another pint, side shot of my song
The song of a long time coming
A man seeking something resembling love
Mentally, emotionally, physically
I sing on

6th drink: My imagination
Where we make love, not sex
On the pool table, then the stage
At your place until sunrise
Why not? Who's to say?

7th drink: Bitter reality, side shot of Jameson
Something to slap me silly
Before I hit the road
Close my tab

8th drink: Water, double
Gotta get home safe
Stay out of trouble

Hope to see you again
Singing like a full moon
Around here real soon

Caffeinding

Double espresso for breakfast

Double espresso for lunch

Double espresso for dinner

Double espresso for dessert
(If I'm a good boy today)

I'm slowly roasting
Into more caffeine
Than man

Late nights and early mornings
Require more than a healthy meal or two

I need a chemical reaction
Heart desires a pulse
I can finally feel
Alive inside

Pick Me Up

I want to pick her up
Sitting there

With words, no muscle
Tongue in cheek

Listen closely

Whispers travel
Only so far

Daring my lips adventure
Across your geography, geometry
As your sensibilities allow
Let down your inhibitions
I tell myself, sitting idle

While you wait, growing impatient
For young man to man older

Make her scream whispers
That travel only so far

Another Round, Please

I drink blonde ales
Intoxicated on brunettes
Pale ales rock my hoppy happiness
While IPAs, like negative energy
Too bitter for my taste buds

Nevertheless, if she's all you got
I'm on top, IPA or not
No bottom for this barrel
My appetite knows no beer bounds

I'll devour you, lager or ale
Whichever seas you sail
Spirits and wines are divine as well
My boat floats to your winds
Any given time of year

Whet my wary whistle
Til the cup overfloweth
Til the cupeth be empty
Suck me dry, my love
My passions and life

Pint by pint
Stine by stine
Ounce by ounce
I'll take you down

Night after night
After night
After next

Titties

Ladies
I want to get
One thing
Off my chest

I love titties

I know I speak for all, most men
When I say this

We love titties

Now, let's not get this twisted (about your titties)
But I thought you aught to know
I'm an admirer, an enthusiast, a devotee
I love me tit-tees

I take solace knowing some women
Love titties, too

Whether they're breasts, boobs
Bazoombas or mosquito bites
They're god's gift to god himself, herself
Whatever god is, I guarantee

God loves titties

Ladies, women
I hope you love your titties
And empower your titties
Behold your titties
Wield your titties
As if the world depends on them

If it weren't for your beautiful titties
World peace would not be possible

Don't get me wrong

IX: You Don't Know Me (You're Welcome)

I love every single square inch
Of your curvatious dimensions
And I'm not just staring
Mouth agape

But damn if a pair of bare titties passing my way
Doesn't have the power
To immediately change my day
For the better

I hope we've not gotten this twisted
About my affinity for titties

Unless, of course
You want me to

Tantra Goddess

Grace my tantra with your subtle touch Love Goddess

I eagerly await the day I attain enlightenment
Past your jade gate, deep within your glorious lotus garden

Allow me to expand and contract, like the flame
Inside deeper dimensions of your breathing

The light of your touch
Seduction from your scent
Bends me and breaks me
In any direction you can erect me

Drunk off the lust upon your tongue
From the valley of those tu-lips
To the precipice of your love button
Let me in

To lap the juices of surrender may be enough for some, but
Baby, I don't come for just anyone

Run your body down my fingertips
Bite your lips into my sin
In between breaths, quicker than death
We lie suspended together in bliss

Tied to the bedposts between the linens of space-time
Let's leave all reservations behind, back at the big bang
When this was only destiny and you were still divine
Tell me, Love Goddess, when did anything change?

For we know too well
Sense too deep

No regrets, no resistance
Only us, you and I, defining our lives
How we like
Scantily

IX: You Don't Know Me (You're Welcome)

Won't you grace my tantra
Expand my consciousness
Guide me to the paradise
Within myself, coiled
Awaiting you

Allow me to release you
Back to the waterfall of kundalini rising
Where none look back on times, or forward
But become one right now
In body and mind

Won't you
Make love
Like you
Love to
Make love
Like you
Love to
Be fucked

Beyond words
Beyond signs
Beyond meanings
Just you and I

United by one love
One tantra

Be forewarned, though

Your OM face
May never be the same again

One Orgasm Per Day

1
An orgasm a day
Keeps the doctor away

An orgasm an hour
Keeps the reaper at bay

2
STOP EJACULATING, GENTLEMEN
Ejaculation and orgasm are not the same

Revere your seed
Like it were the rarest thing
God's good grace bestowed upon thee

No need to succumb
Control your climax
Orgasm all day
Change your world

Choices, choices

3
Ladies
Go nonstop
Gentlemen
Not a drop

Expands her joy
Expresses his health
Look it up, young Taoists
Live long and fornicate often

Longevity is wealth
To the man
At the bottom
Of his health

IX: You Don't Know Me (You're Welcome)

4
Pulse unto breath unto sex
Passion's more powerful than love
Nirvana is fleeting
You wouldn't know a kegel if it kicked you in the perineum
Get close to your pelvic floor
Closer
Before incontinence and boredom overwhelm your bowels
Be the beast your loins deserve
Pulse unto breath unto sex unto death

5
The excess of porn
The masturbation, ejaculation
It's killing us slowly
And women too quickly

Jacking
Whacking
Jerking
Choking
Smacking
Slapping
Beating
Just joking

Subconsciously, men
Self-love's lost its touch

What happened to a good old fashioned rub?

6
Touch yourself
More

Alone
In public
All over
Your body

Because
That's all

7
How to Abhyanga

Ingredients
1 oz. sweet almond oil
6 drops of essential oil (max)

Recipe
- Add essential oils to almond oil; stir
- Warm the oil bottle in a bowl of hot water
- Dispense oil into hand and rub every square inch of your beautiful skin in oil, from crown to sole
    - Notice humorous, sensitive, erogenous zones
    - Recognize any tension you may be carrying
- Massage the oil into your skin for a minimum of 5 minutes; up to 20, if possible
- Take a warm shower and allow the oils to melt into your skin; avoid body wash
- Pat dry

8
Accept your rightful place
Alongside Aphrodite

You are a sexual wonder
Whether you bear the blessing
Or wear the burden

Born of sex sinful
From where we all come
Does that make you sin?
I say no

You are sacred
Accept your orgasmic nature
Embrace the beauty inside your being

I say so, sexy

9
I love my penis

And you should, too
Love your penis

Yes ladies, I want you
To love your penis
Like I love my vagina

I love my vagina

10
Sex positive is not slang for slut
Sex positive is not slang for consent
Sex positive is not slang for fuck's sake
Sex positive is a world we have hardly known
Sex positive is a revolution of the roses
Sex positive is a happy place

Where you confront your sex positively
Neutralizing negativity, internally and externally

Charging every molecule of your soul
With pleasure, accepting ecstasy
As you would your next breath

Inhaling
Exhaling

Pleasure

I Don't Mind

I don't mind
Being that guy
Pen in one hand
Poetry in the other
At the end of the bar
Out drinking you

I don't mind
Being a small man
In a large dudes world
Where my dexterity and speed
Are all I need, I believe
To beat death's nasty bob and weave

I don't mind
Blasting punk rock
Destroying monotony
Creating sacred autonomy
For the sake of future generations
I writhe

I don't mind
Dying in front of millions
For a single laugh

I don't mind
Hiding in the worst of nuclear war
To live the last day

I don't mind
Being the scream of reason
Among whispers day-dreaming

I don't mind
Speaking truth
Hurting feelings
Sucking neck
Taking beatings

IX: You Don't Know Me (You're Welcome)

I don't mind
Your kink, my pleasure
My energy, your weather
You're welcome
I don't mind

I don't mind
Linguistic flings
With an algebraic side-thing

I don't mind
Bending space-time
Pulling ends of the spectrum together
Into a cycle of karma
Breaking the rhyme
Where genius equates madness
And we drink whiskey rye
Until we're blind
By sunrise

I don't mind
Being me uniquely
In a world that doesn't want me
Thinking about defending myself
Sometimes, feels like a breeze to me
Blowing through streets
As easy as a plastic grocery bag
Never to decompose discretely

I don't mind
Improprieties

I forgo niceties
Don't know why

Must be you, maybe

Mind your own

Paper, Please

Paper over plastic
Every day I breathe

Potential over production
People over profits
Action over excuses
Feelings over fears
Truth over dishonesty
Honestly, I'm only human

Votes over violence
Intentions over silence
Life over dying
We're just getting by

And it's getting harder and harder
Each and every day

Air's polluted
Soil's disgraced
Water's poisoned
Planet's hotter every place
Humanity's inconvenienced
Death's a date, not a race

Education over executions
Words over guns
Hugs around everyone
Revolving around the sun

We're responsible
We're capable
We're renewable, but
Don't forget

We're disposable
We fragile humans
No button to reset

Prospects & Opportunities

Can't stop, got hummingbird energy
Same demons, different day
So many hats to wear
Where to begin

Lifelong student
Door-to-door newspaper salesman
Camp counselor-in-training counselor
Barista extraordinaire
Spoken word artist
Weekly open mic creator and host
Liberal studies B.A., Linguistics minor
Theatric sketch-writer
Daylighting-product's swiss-army knife
Husband
Creative arts manager
Poetry small press publisher
Small non-profit executive director
Licensed massage therapist
Screenwriter
Father
Stay-at-home parent
Certified personal trainer
And still so far to go

Hasn't been easy
Wasn't exactly connect the dots
Wouldn't change much
For the best of times come with the worst

Must keep exploring the gardens
Hummingbirds never get bored

Cherish not what's gained or lost
But the memories earned
Moving forward

Hurt

I hurt people
Dearly, sometimes
With nothing more
Than my strongest muscle
My tongue

I can crack my attitude
Wrapped in sarcasm
Laced with personal bite
At 800 miles per hour
In a moments notice

A gift against monsters
A weapon against loved ones

Trigger finger gets ticklish
When I get caught up thinking too much
And then I hurt people
Often on purpose
Sometimes by accident
It's horrible

And I'll do it again
When, and if, I have to

I always have
Always will
Hurt

And in turn
I hurt others
In return

Simulacrum

A father hits his wife in front of his child
Just like his father did, as did his father before him

Now, this son is sitting in detention
For assaulting another child at recess
Because he wanted the ball the boy had
And wasn't about to take no for an answer

Just like his father
The cycle continues

No one saw it begin
The spiral continues on
A paradigm shift like this
Takes a shot stronger than 151
To shake the momentum
Of hollow-point love

No one has any idea
What happened generations ago
We just know what we know
And that's all that we know
And right now, this boy believes
Nothing else really matters
He hates detention

He wants to do something
Destructive
He doesn't know why, but he likes it
Violence

The cycle continues quietly

Adolescence into adulthood
Old age onto the last day
Into the next life
Onto it's first night

The cycle continues, but
Spirals rise and fall in many forms
And what's once a stigma
Becomes the norm

Unwind the time, child
Find peace in knowing you can commit the crime
But understanding the good left behind
By leaving the crime left undone
In your rear-view sights

With some positive conscious change
And a little effort on others' part, who knows
This boy could end up alright
He could go pretty far

If we don't do something soon, though
We can only hope he finds his way
Alone

One Hundred Years Or Bust

I could talk all night about the things that keep me up all day
But there's not enough nights in your lifetime
Nor days left in mine

I've resigned my life to live forever (or as long as possible)
My secrets to longevity?
A few keys

1
Be happy
Uproot the not-happy out of your life
Weed the garden of your mind
Joy is a choice
You behold the hoe
You reep the sow

2
Moderation
Lots of ways to be happy
Lots of ways to be happier
Easy to aim for happier
Harder to come up short
Stay cool, stay calm
Remain copacetic within reason
Suffering loves dis-ease
No need to feed the beast

3
Breathe deep
Dream deeper
Love deepest
Keep it simple

4
Care
Give a damn
Those who stand for nothing
Fall at the feet of fucks

Eyes up, steadfast
You don't cough on dust
All the way up front
Lend a hand before the other man
Because you can

5
Prepare yourself
Nothing is certain
Especially expectations
Bring an extra flamethrower
Just in case your 'hope' don't show
One never knows
When flames will need to be thrown

6
Get alone
Feel yourself
Resign to silence
Learn what it's like
To breathe only yourself in
Senses refined by and by
Deprivation of sensations
By and by yourself

7
Appreciate today
Forgive yesterday
Anticipate tomorrow

8
Don't
Die

9
Repeat daily

[Turn book to Mix Tape #10]

Relationshit

Mix Tape #10

Mix Tape #10
Relationshit

Slow Death

Cold As The Winter Mountain

Spinning

You Got Lucky

Little To Love

Take A Night Off

She Won't Even Spoon In The Wintertime

Where'd She Go?

Just Crystal

One Single Goosebump

Starter Marriage Senioritis

Stop Before Start

Excuses, Excuses

Big You

Without Me

Out Of You

Apathy & We

Why Am I Crying?

Lost Love Memories

I'm Alive

Past Death

Destination Home

Slow Death

Don't fall in love

Don't get married

Don't have children

A family recipe
Passed on
Generation to generation
To kill you
Alive

Cold As The Winter Mountain

Cold as a winter mountain
Her love has fallen quiet
Speaks of no desire, lest fire
A ring was all her heart conspired

Though warmth is hard to come by
I sit idly by, hope for a pyre to burst from her chest, but
Alas, she can't muster more than a pittance of ember

I freeze now, land locked to her hand
On an island all alone surrounded by seas
We don't agree on much lately

Silent, I simply smile along
During tough times in my mind
I seek the sun; it's warmth and optimism
Never can you look down on the sun
Whether it rises or falls on you completely

I seek harmony within myself, without myself
She seeks not

I see the fire in the eyes of those still alive now
She is cold as the winter mountain

Poets are made of more than love, hate, and grace
I sit in zen state, my mind passionately writing
She sits sedate, finding the next great reality show
With which to waste and binge away today

But I shall waste with or without her
With or without myself

Cold as the winter mountain
I burn, baby
And now
It's your turn

Spinning

I would spin
For ever
For you

You can't spin
But once
For me

Cut my oxygen in half again
Watch me dance, lean in
Leave my heart and lungs
Vulnerable
Tease me with breath
One more second
Again

My pain goes unnoticed
Ignored, as you lean away
Further and further
From us

And so
I spin and spin
Endlessly
End less ly
Still waiting
Patiently

Patiently
Fading away
Every rotation
Every revolution
Around this love
I used to call
My sun

You Got Lucky

How does someone become so dense?
How difficult can 'I'm sorry' really be?

Were you raised by baby boomers?

It's the difference between asking and being offered
Demanding and being granted
Welcoming yourself and being invited

I just don't get it sometimes
I just don't get you

Maybe I'm not worth a few minutes of your day
Maybe I'm worth a whole lifetime

Who's to say?

One person's trash
Another's meaning

Here I am cleaning
The pieces of my relationship
Fighting for tomorrow
On the frontlines today

Expletives on my mind
Niceties on my lips

You got lucky, babe
And I?

I got you

You're welcome

Little To Love

Little to love in all the wrong stasis

How does one forget their share
Of uniting two hearts to one timeline

Compromise and affection, attention and convention
Reciprocation and evocation, celebration and appreciation
Basics of relationships that've become taboo here

Like I've disappeared from our relationship
And only my ghost now roams her chest

And it's getting lonely knowing she could care less
And it'll never matter how well I love myself
Without someone to share my flame
Oh well

Now I find little to love, little to nothing
In our tent between the bed sheets
On precious date nights alone
Where once shined fireflies
Now lies quiet hallows

I close my eyes softly
Rest my troubles on concrete pillows
Burning embers dust my skin
Lying next to a heartbeat
That don't beat for me

Take A Night Off

I know I'm not perfect

I know that neither are you

Sorry for the interruption
Any inconvenience

I know you like things
Fair and square

When is it my turn?

I know
I'm far from perfect
C'mon
I'm not close to failure, either

Am I not worth
The benefit of a doubt
Once in a while?

Take a night off

Give me a break

X: Relationshit

She Won't Even Spoon In The Wintertime

As cold as ice, I writhe
Craving affection, I only need a touch of love
One she can't afford to provide

I don't understand what "for better or worse" meant to you
But there are things worse than cuddling up
A hand upon your torso
Our legs intertwined at the hips

She can't give two minutes of conversation
Who am I to ask for such a trivial expectation
On this three hour tour turned island lifetime

Maybe I'm just a fool
And love is just a ruse
Maybe I'll get over this deficiency
And maybe I'll die happy

What's the use?

She won't spoon in the wintertime
You can imagine how bad it gets in the summer

Move over
You're too hot
Get away from me
You're touching too much

As she reaches for heavier blankets
I'm stripped to the bone

What do I know?

It's freezing cold outside these walls
She won't look to me for warmth
Amongst the snow

Where'd She Go?

If I could
I'd love you wild

She won't touch me now
Like she touched me then

I die
Little by little
Without a thought given
Without one received

Where have you gone, girl
Friend, love I once knew

Lust was us
Now outside
I look in
On what was
What may have
Never been
What is
What has yet to be

Undecided
In your right
I die
By the slice
Of your apathy

What is love, anyway?
Besides requited

I'm still waiting

Just Crystal

She keeps me up all night long with little less than a single breath

She gives me that surge of energy I need
Even when awake is not exactly what I'm feeling

She finds a way inside my head
And won't release me until this next thought's left

She's my new intoxication, my new love drug
I always want more, there is no better score

Crystal
Just Crystal

I found her by chance;
One of those funny fates
That only happens
Taking the first step in to dance

She ventured deep inside my eyes
Into my mind and resigned to quiet
Forcing me out from silence

Smiles were shared
Truths were dared
Old scars still linger
Bad skin's been shed

She's my new intoxication, my new love drug

I always want more, and if you knew her, too
You'd know why for sure

She's my new love drug
I'll never give her up

Crystal
Just Crystal

One Single Goosebump

Present yourself to me
Adonis, Aphrodite

I need to know you still find me
Attractive, addictive, anything
Everything I used to do to you
Maybe that's just history now

Your body bounces and flickers
Vibrant like a candle flame still
For once bear your bare body
Before me, for me, my love

I need to know
You'd still love
To love me

In dreams or reality
I need to know our spark
Isn't only in my eyes

Give yourself to me
Completely
For once
Be my fantasy
Discretely

No one needs to know
How we unwrap each other
In ecstasy, in our bed sheets
Our secret, you and me

Surprise us both

Let go

Take me with you

Starter Marriage Senioritis

It's not that the dream is over
The fantasy's dead

Big difference

What once was com-passionate
Has been replaced with sleep
Unwilling, unassuming
Unavoidable at best

Such is the fate of a man
Bore into dire circumstances
Balancing internal prioritizations
On a high-wire of her expectations

To receive so little seems absurd
Giving more than I possess
Not asking for much, instead
I'm made the fool of burden
By comparison of our breads

It's not the fantasy that's dead
It's the sex, or the marriage
Whichever is worse
Haven't figured that out yet

Oh, who's this poem kidding?
Sweet dreams, sweet dreamers

May your rocks run melted
And your hearts bleed rose red

May your fantasies come true
And your screams graze the moon

Stop Before Start

Stop giving yourself that hope
She don't care

Stop hoping she'll be there for you
She's not there

Stop thinking it's gonna get better
She won't dare

Stop making yourself more depressed
She can't fair

In the end
I own the pain
She don't give fucks
She don't care
She just takes up
Space on the couch
Time on the wifi
As I waste away

Stop hoping
She'll be there
And make it better

She's not one for relationships
Just Housewives of wherever

Let down
Again and again

When will I learn
Not to listen
To the consummate optimist
In my head

She wants him dead

Excuses, Excuses

What's the excuse tonight?

Haven't shaved? Haven't showered?
Ate Mexican food?
Too tired?

What's it tonight, babe?

Just not feeling it?
Too hot out? Too cold?
I haven't shaved?
I'm a fucking asshole?

What's up tonight?

Bring me breaking news
Not just excuses renewed
For another season of reruns
I want something original, hun

I'm all ears burning, and
You're just pages, chapters
Not turning my softcover
Hard on the bestseller list

I howl to the moon
Night in, night out
Does me no good

Excuses, excuses
All I ever get

Don't mind me

I'm always in the mood

Big You

Don't worry
No one's expecting
You to be
The bigger man

Nowadays
You can choose
To be
The bigger woman

We don't
Discriminate ignore-ance
By sex or gender
Anymore

Be bigger
Be better
Beginning
Yesterday

We appreciate it
Tomorrow

Without Me

Is it bad
That sometimes
I imagine life
Without you?

Not that we're
Not together
No, I imagine
You dead

Is that bad?

Perfectly normal?

Either way
I'd rather you
Alive

Is that best?

Out Of You

I want out

Out of your heart
Out of your eye
Out of your hand
Out of your mind

I want out

Out of this
Out of this shit
Out of this shit we go through
Out of this shit

I want out

I don't want it anymore
I don't need this

I want to taste a fresh breath again
I want to laugh like I used to again
I want to feel alive for the first time again
I want to feel like myself, again

I don't need this
I want out

I don't need this
I need out

I don't need you

I'm out
Down and out

Where do I go from here?

Apathy & We

How do we become so numb
To the ones we love?

Like they're pincushions
Ready to carry the weight of our nails

We wouldn't treat strangers that way
Would we?

How does one become what they hate
Besides hating what they're become?

Sharp tongues need not apply here
Soft hearts welcome 24/7

We are human beings
We lovers

Compassion incapacitated
Resuscitation required

We need a straight shot
Stronger than words exactly

Where does one find one million volts
To blow out the apathy?

Why Am I Crying?

I've never cried more
In my entire life

Since falling in love
Getting married
Having children
Mortality rising
Or all the above

One delicate emotion

Punches in waves
Slices to the vein

Damn
What the most important
Things in your world
Can get away with

I've never cried more
In my entire life

No need to hide
Those Disney films now
Get me every time

Lost Love Memories

There's no getting back
The nothing we never had

It's lost, it's gone
It once was, but now
Long forgotten

Fading in time
Like light from the day
Never getting away
No keeping it in place

The more we fight, the stronger it embraces
Lesser it leaves us with, the more we gain

Love is energy
Easy to transform
Easy to mold, but
Impossible to destroy

Sometimes, I think I want to go back
Give these lessons a second try
But more often times I realize, I remember
How happy I am with one shot

I wouldn't wish myself
Upon anyone else
It's a gift, a blessing
I thank you for this

For the lessons learned
In all your fire

I thank you

I'm Alive

My pulse
May have skipped
A few hundred beats

My eyes
May have closed
For more than
A few years wink

My life
May flash before me
A few frames longer
Than reincarnation imagined

No matter, all energy
I am alive

You may have thought
You drained me of love
But honey, I've got reserves
Enough for everyone

The closer I got
To the end of the well
The stronger my desire
To climb upward out of hell

You opened my life
In reverse, nice try
Good luck getting me back
Inside my casket

No tragedy
All integrity
I'm alive, baby

I'm alive

Past Death

I'm sorry
You are not
Like everyone else

You are my love
The lengths I'd live for you
Incomparable
To any other human alive

I cannot deny
My love runs deep
Past the core of the Earth
Into parallel universes

Generations of rivers
Have carried my bones
Downstream for eternity
Unto your blood, unto yours

The lengths I'd go
Immeasurable
In physical terms
Every pain worthy

It's an unreal truth
You will one day learn
Bringing life to this world

Destination Home

I couldn't see myself
With anyone else

I can't believe I am
Blessed to have found you

I won't leave this gift
Without giving my own present

I wouldn't trade this
This life, love, and strife
For anything

Thank you
For being here
Thick and thin
Angel and bitch

I can be a handful, myself, sometimes
Wouldn't change a thing
Seems like neither will you
So predictable

Without you
I'd only be floating alone
With no one, no where
To keep me tethered
Down to the ground
I call home

Call me home
For once, once again

Call me home
Back to us

[Turn book to Mix Tape #11]

Thoughts of a Lost Dreamer

Mix Tape #11

Mix Tape #11
Thoughts of a Lost Dreamer

Dirty Romantic

Why Not?

In the Music

Scar Stories

Love Disease

Dreaming Behind The Wheel

Poetry Copter

Swing

Kiss Me (Between Blinking)

Speak To Me

Why I Can't Wake Up At Six In The Morning

Last Takeoff

Untitled (Re-Vision)

To My Unborn Wonder

"Thoughts of a Lost Dreamer", the complete chapbook
1st appeared in iWrite: Words & Voices (2014)
by Poetry In Motion Publishing House

Dirty Romantic

I'm a dirty romantic

I fall in love too easily with the architecture of back alleys
I live amongst the treetops, tower over skyscrapers at sunrise
I dream from the womb of the oxygen in my near future
And there's nothing anyone can do about it

I'm a dirty romantic

Dancing for rain naked through midnight streets
Blowing etheric smoke rings nag champa
I am revolutionizing the art of breathing deeply
And refusing, refuting any rumors I've gone hipster

There's no greater threat to our way of life
Than corporations and hipsters

Call me what you will
Except corporate or hipster, because
I'm a dirty romantic, and you
Don't have a death wish

I practice dirty romanticism daily
Don't get in my way; that's a warning
I've got waves to make, tides to carry away
All semblance of hope lost, in humanity found
Swimming against the rip to get closer to your shore

I'm a dirty romantic
Not even my parents could do anything about that

You've been forewarned: I'm coming for you
Prepare yourself for my love

I'm a dirty, dirty romantic

Tell me, how do you like it?

Why Not?

I just wanna watch every sunrise
I just wanna dance anytime there's music on nearby
I just wanna love every lady leg that passes my way
I just wanna love my lady like the first time, every time
For the rest of our lives together

I just wanna be a man
I just wanna be a man's man
I just wanna be a ladies man
I just wanna be a man other men, women, little children remember
Long after I'm dust let loose to the wind

I just wanna burn
I just wanna leave nothing behind
I just wanna punk rock-it all the fucking time
I just wanna unapologize

I just wanna blow your mind
I just wanna fuck your sex
I just wanna graze your neck, bubble you in goosebumps
I just wanna powder you in mist from within
Then leave your lungs breathless for another 60 minutes

I just wanna love you
I just wanna love me, too
I just wanna love to love
I just wanna love to be loved like you

I just wanna be a little wiser than I was only yesterday
I just wanna be a little better the next opportunity I get
I just wanna make our little world a worthwhile place
To raise my daughters in
And I just wanna watch every sunset

I don't think that's too much to ask for
Why?

I just wanna

In The Music

When the music's loud
And when the music's good
And when the music's good and loud
There's nowhere else to be

Out of your seat, out of your mind
When it's good and loud and it's got you
There's nowhere, no one, no nothing
That really fucking matters

Turn me on
Turn it up
Let it loose
Let me in

One foot to the ground
The other anywhere else
Both hands deep inside the ether
Hips infused to the wind

I burn with desire
A spark amongst the fire
Hold a flame in place for one moment
It's impossible, not really logical
Audience unstoppable
Why leave now?

When the music's good
And when the music's loud
When the music's got you
And you've let go
Completely
Willingly
There's only one question left

Care to dance?

Scar Stories

9 stitches
4 fractured bones
1 concussion
6 separate instances
And a whole lot more to go, I am
Only getting started

Walking at 8 months old, I was on the move
Ready for adventure, a young man's legacy left to prove
Not two months later, running about
I tripped—hit my head on the VCR corner hard
Found myself with gushing blood, rushed for two stitches
A third eye lighting bolt from that moment until this
I'm talking about scar stories

Speaking volumes more than iTunes collection or vacation photos
Who knows where we'd be without these tales of the flesh
During moments in elevators without anything to talk about
How awkward without a scar story in your back pocket

How sad how simple, how safe your life would be

Get hurt, know pain

There will come a day you only wish you were still alive
Waking up once again in the after light
Hell without action, every moment unknown
Taking chances by the throat

We note the fact of these happenings called accidents
There's a whole world daring us to keep pace, follow after
But we never knew no better than the chase
As we uncovered the Mohs of blacktop asphalt
The unforgiveness of gravity
Hypothesized the breaking point of human flesh, then
Went on to discover how many licks it takes
To get to the center of connective tissue

XI: Thoughts of a Lost Dreamer

My body has stories to tell
Some more unbelievable than the scars will admit
They're humble like that
Help me remember myself sometimes
Every time they come to mind
Remind me, more so
Than vacation photos or iTunes collections
I am more than memories

I am resilience

In every ounce of opportunity a pinch of danger
But that's why we like it, right?
Life, living, love, losing

No matter how many times we fall
We fall
And we get up once again
Dying to feel weightlessness once more

Staring into night skies so deep
We need the starlight
Just to keep us grounded

Tell me about
Your most gnarly scars
Visible or not

I'd like to get to know you better
Through tales of your sacred temple
Not your measly day job or today's weather
I want to experience touch together

You have a tale to tell

Where do you begin?

Love Disease

If eye contact were a disease
You'd swear I'd be HIV

I can't help it
I need to see you
The shine of your pupil
The light inside your mind
I need to feel you
I can't fake it
Communication
Otherwise

Let's hold right there
Where attention stands ready
And neither end will let go

Let's hold right here
Standing attentive, steadily
Clinging to this moment
Unspoken

If eye contact were a disease
You'd swear I'd be
Dead by now

I contracted an infection
I refused to be cured of
Whatever you do, beware
Vampires roam everywhere

I'm the last thing you see coming
Until it's too late
Don't wait too long, it only takes a glance
Before you're already gone

Was it good for you?
Good
Bye

Dreaming Behind The Wheel

I dream of the day smiles shine brighter
Laughter becomes currency
Dreams manifest into reality, and
I finally catch my breath

I dream of the day sons are allowed to be themselves
Daughters are comfortable in their own skin
Parents live to raise their children
Not the other way around

I dream of the day complete strangers become comrades
Families sit together and discuss the power of silence
Mother Earth returns to her rightful role as goddess
I dream of this day

I dream of the day coffee is free and gasoline is non-existent
Love is traded on the stock market, corporations are not people
Television has no agenda, entertainment is thought-provoking
Internet is sewn into our fingers, starvation is non-existent
Disease is no longer our fate, and cancer is preventable

I dream of the day you and I continue on without end
You and I touch without physical interaction
You and I find ourselves inseparable
Welcome everywhere, any time

I dream of the day harmony takes form
Synchronicity is finally achieved
I dream of the day we follow our chi
Find the tao inside every living thing

I dream of the day we have nothing left to dream of
Because every day, every moment
We be just as we should

A fantasy without limitation
A reality beyond our imagination

Poetry Copter

Let's get one thing straight

I don't appreciate you assuming
I like doing this poetry thing

It's a labor of lust

I don't do it for anyone but myself
Still, I get the feeling you get me
You get something from this
You get it

A fleeting feeling
A newfound thought
A deeper wound
A tighter stomp

I know what you're thinking, you're thinking
"I bet he does this for the riches, the bitches"
But no, I do this because poetry itches the inside of my skull
All day, every day, and I can't get away from myself long enough
It's hell

Might fly off the shelves
Tomorrow
Might be on the black market
Today

I could care less

When it's bad, it's good
When it's worse, it's better
When it's left unwritten, that's the best
Don't ever get mistaken

Ink never forgets

While I sit here in a coffee shop

XI: Thoughts of a Lost Dreamer

Early in the morning
As my mind decides the next line
I'm set to write
I ask myself

Where have I gone?
Where have I come from?
How do I plan on getting back?
And why would I ever want to!

Let's get one thing straight

I didn't choose to start writing poetry
No, poetry chose to ride with me

Keeps me up at night
At this same damn coffee shop
Wondering
'What was poetry thinking?'

I question his credibility

Swing

I see you got that something in your eye, child
But one day, you better realize you still got that hook
Because you look at where you're jabbing, but blabbing
I'm still standing right here in front of you

I wanna see what you're made of

In the ring, the whites of your eyes have gone red
Breathing heavily, head held high, you're not yet dead
Still, you got both your dukes up in front of your face
Hiding the disgrace of too many punches thrown
And a whole lot of nothing landed

So now, it's time to change it up a bit
Maybe deviate from what'cha been up'ta
It's time to shake it up a bit, maybe
See what it is you're made of

Because if you quit now
You're just gonna be down and out, and
Right now, you've got the fight of your life
Standing right here in front of you

Truth be told, every underdog gets themselves there somehow

So what do you say?
You gonna go ahead and let me make my day
Or are you gonna do something, anything about it
To bring about some change?
I wanna know

Because if you're still standing
You've got more than you would
From down there on the floor

So go ahead

Swing

Kiss Me (Between Blinking)

Kiss me
Again
With that
Look

I know
You've got
That look
Inside you

When eyes
Meet eyes
Or lips
Meet lips
It is
A kiss
One cannot
Envisage

One can
Only fashion
Such things
Through
Union

Prove to me
Right here
Right now
That light
In you
Shining
When I
Find you
Inside
Yourself
Is real

Prove me

Right

Kiss me
Again
With that
One look

Appears
Your gaze
Could kill
If warranted

Kiss me
Kill me
Whatever
You do
Don't leave
Me breathing

You've
Got
Lust
In you

You've got
Me in you

Don't look now

I've got you
In me too

And then
We blink
Without
Goodbye

Speak To Me

Speak to me in words
Words I have never heard before
Before I ever met you here
Here in real life

I find everyone singing noise
Noise with no substance, no truth
Truth beyond a reasonable doubt
Doubt full of sounds screamed aloud

Believe me, I was only sleeping
Dreaming of a life within your love
Trusting the winds and where they send us
Bound to weightlessness
Completely

Compassion in our shoulders
Light in the soles of our feet
A smile in our bellies
Mind teeming with potential
And a song inside our seat

Speak to me
In words
I have never
Heard before

Your voice will be
The life of me

Why I Can't Wake Up At Six In The Morning

If I do
The evil monsters will get me

If I do
World peace will continue
To not exist

If I wake up at six in the morning
The universe collapses

That's a warning you can take to the grave
And I wouldn't let me sleep in on it

I can stay up
Until 6 in the morning

I can stir at 6 in the morning
Only to hit snooze
But never shall I awake
At 6 a.m.

If I do
The Mayans
Will have been right
The entire time

Don't let me catch the worm
I've got zzz's to chase down

If I don't
This bus will explode

Give me just another few minutes of fuse to burn

I don't want to sleep through
Destroying the world

Imagine

Last Takeoff

It's like they knew we were going to die

They aren't usually overly charismatic
Telling us the safety information before takeoff
But this time seemed a little more like
Why even bother?

Once we took off
I had a funny feeling about this flight
I say so to myself every time we launch into the sky
But this has never before felt so right

We hit ten-thousand feet
The electronic device light turned off
The seat belt sign stayed on
Then, all of a sudden, just silence

Terminal velocity on every side
Nose diving to the end of our lives
In slow motion, faster than any of us has ever fallen
We were all sullen in our descent

The oxygen masks never fell
Our life preservers were no good
The crew continued serving drinks and food
And I simply kept writing poetry

It's all that I could do

Untitled (Re-Vision)

I devise, I rewrite
Tear it apart, then
Start all over again

I find I go
Nowhere fast
Often easily

Caught up in my mind
Indecisive by design, I try
To find direction for no destination
An electron lost amongst the equation

How does one know
What they are looking for
When their quest is
Undefined; an answer
Man made as time

I devise, I rewrite
Tear it apart, then
Make it right

To do better
No matter
Rising above
The letter of grammar

Always tomorrow
A new man
Revised

I am far
From finished

To My Unborn Wonder

Dear unborn
Son or daughter

I eagerly await
The moment I meet you

Before you're old enough
To become disenfranchised
By the world-at-large
Please, remember this

In no particular order

Be yourself
You don't owe anyone anything, besides yourself
Speak your mind
Embrace the silence and chaos that surround you
Listen passionately
Dream emphatically
Entertain time-tested wisdom as if it were new-fangled fashion
Question mediocrity
Take at least one deep breath hourly
Discover your center
Learn from every mistake
Take chances by the throat
Find God
Trust your instincts
Go with the flow
Love your family, humanity
Denounce discrimination
Weed the garden of your mind
Nurture your spirit
Meditate once in a while
Drink lots of water
Enjoy the little things
Act as if all moments are perfect
Kiss your crush
Marry your soul mate

Sing, dance, and fuck fast, loud, and safely
Practice daily life without restraint
Deviate from preconceived notions
Let no one stop you from destiny
Be the change, for better or worse
Invest time in good karma
Desire nothing
Peace comes from within
Respect posture
Hold the future hostage
Appreciate nature
Go ask your mother
Take your time
Optimism is your greatest ally
Sleep is an illusion
Culture is the enemy
I will let you down at times
Experiment with daily life
Everything's negotiable
Celebrate your youth while you can
You're going to go to college; start planning now
If you make a promise, keep it
Hard work pays off
Age is not a curse
Don't look back
Don't let anyone else carry your flag
Second chances are not guaranteed
Always choose love

Please remember this

Before you become disenfranchised
By the world-at-large

I love you

And there's nothing you can do about it

See you soon

About the Author

Jason Brain, Poet

Jason Brain's passion is breathing. When he's not breathing, Jason can be found writing and performing poetry around the Southern California area; delivering professional massage bodywork with Brain & Body Massage; enjoying some of his creative hobbies including photography and screenwriting; and spending quality time at home with his family.

Creator of the weekly open mic, Soapbox Sessions, running in the San Fernando Valley since 2006, Jason also enjoys anything having to do with sports, philosophizing with friends, laughing and dancing out loud, and the company of coffee at sunrise and beer at sunset.

He hopes to meet you soon.

www.jasonbrain360.com

ALSO BY JASON BRAIN:
Mix Tape Collection: Original Poetry
Poetry In Motion Publishing House, 2012

Songs in the Key of Revolution: Mix Tape Collection II
Poetry In Motion Publishing House, 2016

www.ingramcontent.com/pod-product-compliance
Lightning Source LLC
LaVergne TN
LVHW041631070426
835507LV00008B/554